The Art of
Giving Flowers

The Art of
Giving Flowers

Callie Craumer

Drawings by Fiona Kwan

Published by Prospecta Press
An imprint of Easton Studio Press
P.O. Box 3131
Westport, CT 06880
(203) 454-4454
www.prospectapress.com

Book design by Nancy Mazzoli
Cover design by Barbara Aronica-Buck

Hardcover ISBN 978-1-935212-72-0
E-book ISBN 978-1-935212-71-3

First edition

Printed in Canada
First printing: February 2012

To

Nancy, without whose dedication
this book would not be possible,

and
Ernie, who redefined the meaning
of a part-time job

Contents

Garden Rose

Introduction

Flowers make people happy and are a perfect gift for any occasion.

Flowers have an immediate impact on happiness, a long-term positive effect on moods, and increase the connections among family and friends. One of the greatest benefits to giving flowers is flowers make people happy.

– Dr. Jeannette Haviland-Jones, Rutgers University

Gerbera Daisy

This guide will help you become a better educated consumer. It's a quick reference that includes all the basic tools you need to understand the simple art of giving flowers. You will learn not only how to use flowers to express your feelings more effectively but also how to get what you want. You will be more confident when you purchase flowers on the Internet, over the phone, or in person at a local flower shop.

As you become more familiar with the most basic elements of a flower arrangement – color, flower meaning, reason for giving, style, and design – you can more effectively communicate your needs to a florist. This will help you get what you want.

If you are buying flowers for yourself, you are more likely to be happy with your selection, and with a few simple tips on flower care you can enjoy them a little longer.

Hydrangea

When ordering flowers, have the recipient's name, complete address, and phone number available, as well as your message and payment information.

I. Flower Color

Understanding the meaning and principles of color can help you express your feelings or complement the personality of the recipient.

*Choose the recipient's favorite color —
it's a great place to start.*

The Meaning of Flower Color

Agapanthus

White	Innocence, Elegance, Peace, Purity
Yellow	Happiness, Friendship, Enthusiasm
Orange	Energy, Passion, Confidence
Red	Love, Passion, Strength, Desire
Pink	Gentleness, Grace, Youth
Purple	Dignity, Pride, Success
Lavender	Femininity, Grace, Admiration
Blue	Openness, Peace, Serenity
Green	Life, Fortune, Youth, Optimism

The Principles of Color

The color wheel is a tool that illustrates the relationship of colors. Many different color combinations work well to achieve beautiful floral arrangements.

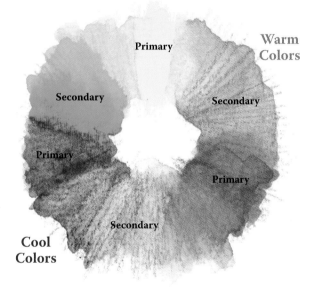

When selecting flowers, don't ever hesitate to choose your own favorite color.

The Language of Color

Primary
Red, yellow, and blue
are the principal colors.

Secondary
Mixing two primary colors
together makes purple,
orange, or green.

Complementary
Opposite, high-contrast tones
like blue and orange, red and green,
or yellow and purple create
energizing combinations.

Adjacent
These are the colors close to each
other on the color wheel, like
green and yellow, orange and red,
and blue and purple. Use two or
more touching colors together
to produce a subtle effect.

Warm
Shades of yellow, orange,
and red are vivid and full
of energy, like the sun.

Cool
Green, blue, and purple
shades create a calm, soothing,
and relaxing feeling.

Color Combinations

It helps to know the vocabulary florists use to describe the most common color combinations in flower arrangements.

Lily of the Valley

Monochromatic
One color or the range of a single color, with or without the addition of greens, creates a simple or modern look. White, cream, and ivory create a clean, sophisticated, and elegant effect. Shades of pink reflect a feminine palette. Orange hues communicate energy and vibrancy.

Aster

Polychromatic
Combinations of many colors like red, blue, purple, yellow, orange, hot pink, and bright green produce whimsical, cheerful arrangements.

When it comes to color, let your natural creativity be your guide.

> *Choose an abundance of one type of flower or all one color for a simple statement.*

Pastels
Soft colors in shades of pink, peach, lavender, pale yellow, pale blue, and cream can be used for a subdued appearance.

Sweetpea

Jewel Tones
Gold, purple, fuchsia, and dark blue are the strong colors of this palette. Imagine the look of a beautiful stained glass window for a rich and elegant statement.

Country French
Vibrant shades of violet, blue, orange, yellow, and red give a rustic garden appearance.

Freesia

Seasonal

Spring	Soft pastel colors
Summer	Bright, strong colors
Fall	Warm hues of yellow, gold, orange, red, and green
Winter	Cool, clean tones of white, red, green, and blue

Send a Message with Color

Specific colors are associated with the message you want to send.

Chrysanthemum

Admiration	Purple
Celebration	Bright, bold colors
Friendship	Yellow
Love and Passion	Red, pink, purple, and orange
Optimism	Green
Patriotism	Red, white, and blue
Relaxation	Green and blue
Serenity	White and pastels
Success	Orange
Sympathy	White or peach

II. Flower Meaning

Traditionally, many flowers have a special meaning, which may influence the varieties of flowers you choose.

The Meaning of Common Flowers

Agapanthus
   Love

Agapanthus

Alstroemeria
   Friendship
   Fortune
   Aspiration

Alstroemeria

Aster
   Patience
   Daintiness
   Love

Aster

Baby's Breath
Happiness
Innocence

Baby's Breath

Birds of Paradise
Magnificence
Joyfulness

Birds of Paradise

Calla Lily
Beauty
Magnificence

Calla Lily

Choose a flower you like even if its meaning doesn't convey exactly what you want to say.

Carnation
- Pink   Gratitude
- Red   Admiration, Passion
- White   Innocence, Remembrance
- Yellow Pure Love, Cheerfulness

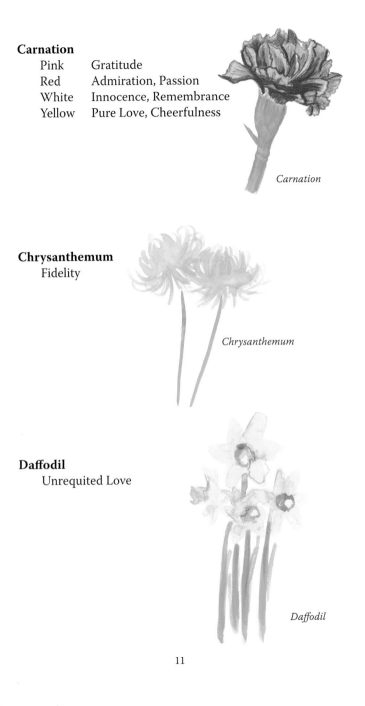

Carnation

Chrysanthemum
- Fidelity

Chrysanthemum

Daffodil
- Unrequited Love

Daffodil

*Give extra thought to the card message.
It is a wonderful opportunity to add
a wow factor to your gift of flowers.*

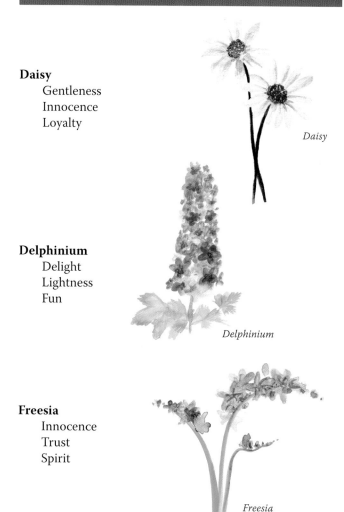

Daisy
    Gentleness
    Innocence
    Loyalty

Daisy

Delphinium
    Delight
    Lightness
    Fun

Delphinium

Freesia
    Innocence
    Trust
    Spirit

Freesia

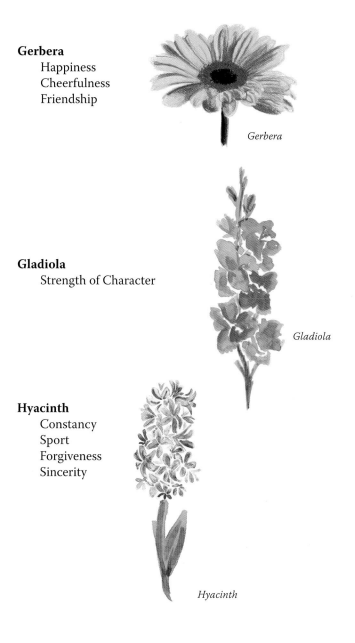

Gerbera
    Happiness
    Cheerfulness
    Friendship

Gerbera

Gladiola
    Strength of Character

Gladiola

Hyacinth
    Constancy
    Sport
    Forgiveness
    Sincerity

Hyacinth

Hydrangea
Understanding
Perseverance
Vanity

Hydrangea

*Use your imagination when choosing flowers;
the possibilities are limitless and
most flowers are available year-round.*

Iris
Faith
Wisdom
Inspiration

Iris

Larkspur
Attachment
Beautiful Spirit

Larkspur

Lilac
   Youthful Innocence

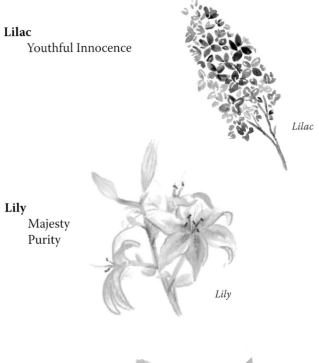

Lilac

Lily
   Majesty
   Purity

Lily

Lily of the Valley
   Purity
   Sweetness

Lily of the Valley

*Green flowers or foliage are considered
neutral and can be used freely with all colors.*

Lisianthus
  Calm

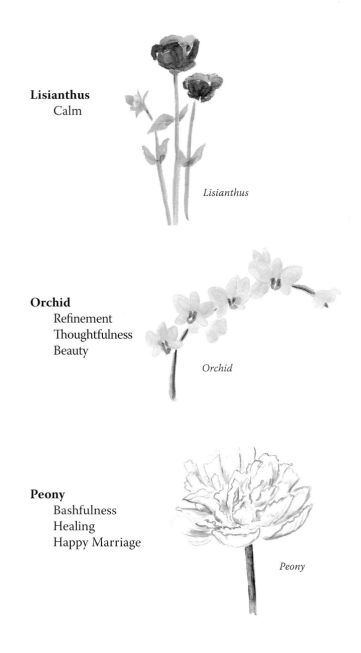

Lisianthus

Orchid
  Refinement
  Thoughtfulness
  Beauty

Orchid

Peony
  Bashfulness
  Healing
  Happy Marriage

Peony

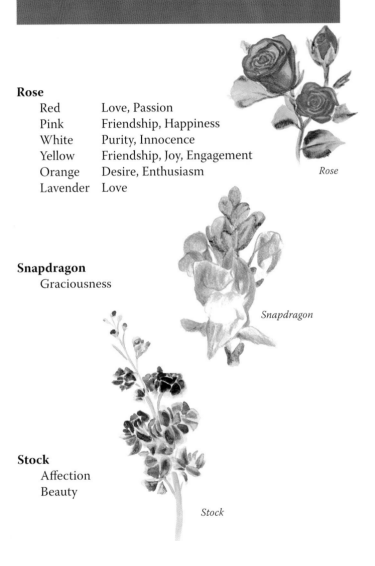

Say "I Love You" with a single red rose.

Rose

Red	Love, Passion
Pink	Friendship, Happiness
White	Purity, Innocence
Yellow	Friendship, Joy, Engagement
Orange	Desire, Enthusiasm
Lavender	Love

Rose

Snapdragon
Graciousness

Snapdragon

Stock
Affection
Beauty

Stock

Sunflower
  Purity
  Devotion
  Pride

Sunflower

Sweet Pea
  Pleasure
  Shyness

Sweet Pea

Thistle
  Nobility
  Austerity

Thistle

Tulip
  Love
  Fame

Tulip

III. Flowers for Special Occasions

These are the most common reasons and occasions for giving flowers.

Rose

Anniversary	**I'm Sorry**
Birth	**Love**
Congratulations	**Sympathy**
Get Well	**Thank You**
Happy Birthday	**Thinking of You**

Give flowers to thank someone for a job well done or to strengthen an important business relationship.

A Flower for Each Birthday Month

January	Carnation
February	Iris
March	Daffodil
April	Sweet Pea
May	Lily
June	Rose
July	Larkspur
August	Gladiola
September	Aster
October	Marigold
November	Chrysanthemum
December	Narcissus

Larkspur

An unexpected gift of flowers always gets special attention and makes people happy.

A Flower for Each Anniversary Year

Tulip

Don't forget that men like flowers, too.

First	Carnation	**Eleventh**	Tulip
Second	Lily of the Valley	**Twelfth**	Peony
Third	Sunflower	**Thirteenth**	Chrysanthemum
Fourth	Hydrangea	**Fourteenth**	Orchid
Fifth	Daisy	**Fifteenth**	Rose
Sixth	Calla Lily	**Twentieth**	Aster
Seventh	Freesia	**Twenty-fifth**	Iris
Eighth	Lilac	**Thirtieth**	Lily of the Valley
Ninth	Birds of Paradise	**Fortieth**	Gladiola
Tenth	Daffodil	**Fiftieth**	Yellow Rose

Widely Celebrated Holidays

Often holidays bring to mind special memories. Here are the colors of flowers associated with some of those important occasions.

New Year's Eve – December 31
All white or jewel tones with accents in silver and gold create an air of celebration.

Valentine's Day – February 14
Red, pink, and purple bring to mind feelings of romance and signify love.

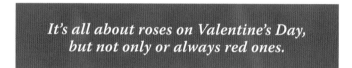

It's all about roses on Valentine's Day, but not only or always red ones.

St. Patrick's Day – March 17
Green carnations and Bells of Ireland are popular for this special day.

Easter – March or April
Soft, pastel colors and bulb flowers like hyacinths, tulips, and daffodils signify the start of spring.

Daffodils

Administrative Professionals' Day – April

A bright, colorful arrangement is the perfect way to acknowledge a job well done.

Mother's Day – Second Sunday of May

For one of the most celebrated days, choose Mom's favorite color or flower to let her know you are thinking about her.

Hydrangea

Memorial Day – Last Monday of May

Bright colors signal the start of summer, especially blue.

Father's Day – Third Sunday of June

Give bright primary colors or Dad's favorite flower to show him how important he is.

Fourth of July – July 4

Red, white, and blue makes a patriotic statement.

Thanksgiving – Fourth Thursday of November

Warm, autumnal flowers accented by gourds, pumpkins, and leaves mark the fall season.

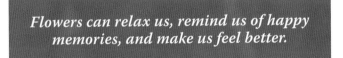

Flowers can relax us, remind us of happy memories, and make us feel better.

Christmas – December 25

Scented winter greens with red and white flowers, berries, and pinecones suggest a winter wonderland.

Sympathy

Flowers are a thoughtful way to honor the passing of a loved one. Many people choose flowers or colors that remind them of or express the personality of the deceased. A florist can always help you if you are uncertain about what to choose.

> *Families genuinely like to receive a gift of flowers when they have lost a relative or a friend. It can lift their spirits.*

Funeral Vase or Wicker Basket
Flowers in a vase or basket
are an appropriate expression
of sympathy.

Traditional Funeral Basket
A fan-shaped floral arrangement
with an assortment of flowers
and foliage sends your message
of sympathy.

Gladiola

Standing Funeral Spray
A funeral arrangement on an easel comes
in a variety of styles, shapes, and sizes that
may include a basic spray, wreath, heart,
or cross, and is often used for a funeral
or memorial service.

IV. Flowers with Special Characteristics

Fragrant Flowers

There are a handful of flowers with a pleasant scent that may have a soothing or memorable quality. Be aware that some people like fragrant flowers while others do not.

> *If the arrangement is going to be used on a table where food is being served, you may not want to choose flowers that have a scent.*

Carnation
Freesia
Hyacinth
Lilac
Lily
Lily of the Valley
Peony
Rose (some varieties)
Stock
Sweet Pea

Lilac

> *If you suspect that someone may be allergic to flowers, avoid sending lilies.*

Longer-Lasting Flowers

If longevity is your primary objective, these flowers tend to last longer than many others, typically seven to ten days.

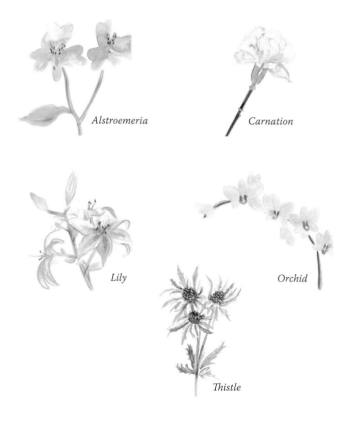

Alstroemeria

Carnation

Lily

Orchid

Thistle

Be sure to change the water often to maximize the life of all flowers.

Flowering Bulbs

There are a few bulb flowers that are available primarily in the spring as either plants or cut flowers. They are often bright and colorful, signifying the beginning of the season.

Bulb flowers have a shorter life when sold as cut flowers.

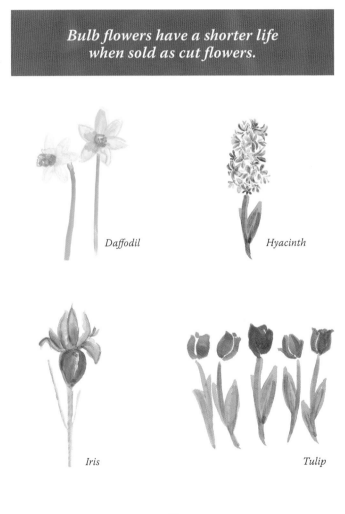

Daffodil

Hyacinth

Iris

Tulip

Winter Greens

A large assortment of seasonal greens and berries are readily available during the winter. They make beautiful arrangements on their own or can be used in combination with flowers.

The scent of winter greens often brings to mind memories of the holiday season.

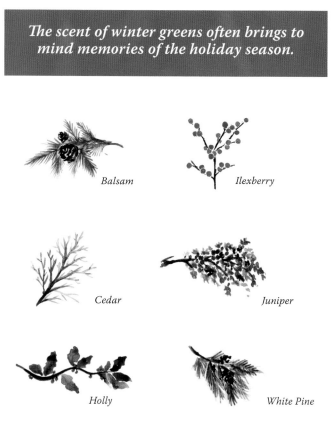

Balsam

Ilexberry

Cedar

Juniper

Holly

White Pine

A simple basket of winter greens with accents of pinecones and berries makes a delightful seasonal arrangement.

V. Simple Flower Design

Florists use common terms to describe the appearance or design of an arrangement. To help get the look you want, become familiar with this vocabulary.

The Vocabulary of Design

Informal
Simple and casual, this style uses a wide range of colors and flowers that are uncomplicated.

Spray Rose

Traditional
This classic style is usually made up of a variety of flowers and colors that are commonly used together and are easy to understand.

A leaf, beargrass, or branches placed inside the container adds drama, hides stems, and disguises the mechanics of the arrangement.

Natural

Loose and airy, open and informal, with a variety of green foliage, this style has the look of flowers just picked from the garden.

Delphinium

Big and Showy

Size is the main objective; the type of flower is not as important. Less expensive flowers, abundant greens, and filler flowers are used to make the arrangement appear larger.

Romantic

Romantic arrangements usually consist of soft, pastel colors in an unstructured design, often with the addition of a subtle fragrance.

Hydrangea

Pavé

Low and compact with minimal greens, this style is often used for centerpieces. Based on the flower selection, these arrangements can be either traditional or contemporary in feeling.

Specialty

A specialty arrangement is one that captures personal memories through design with materials that highlight the characteristics of a person, place, or thing.

In a pavé style, the flowers support each other so they are less likely to wilt and, therefore, will last longer.

Elegant and Sophisticated

This design uses simple lines and fewer types of flowers that are often of better quality and, therefore, have a higher perceived value.

Minimalist

Referred to as high-style, modern, or architectural, this design often has fewer, more dramatic elements and can be very trendy or unconventional.

Lily of the Valley

Organic

Casual and earthy in appearance, these arrangements are unstructured and unconventional with foliage, organic material, and elements like rocks, berries, pods, and woodland accents. The container can be unique and is often a significant part of the design.

An arrangement will stay in place in the container if the stems are tied together.

Anthurium

Exotic
Tropical or less common flowers, which often include orchids, can be used creatively in unusual combinations of color and shape.

Aspidistra

Spiral Bouquet
This kind of bouquet positions the stems in a circular design or pattern that can be seen inside a glass vase. It has the advantage of a design inside and outside of the container.

Nosegay
A small bouquet of flowers, with or without a vase, can be the perfect, thoughtful gift. It is often hand-tied so the flowers stay in place.

Agapanthus

All-Around
Most arrangements will be designed this way unless you request something else. Basically, it will look the same from all sides, perfect for a center hall table.

Three-Sided
This arrangement is often placed against a wall and is designed to be seen from the front and sides.

VI. Arrangement Composition

By understanding the relative size, the basic flower shapes, and the style of the container, you can more easily imagine the look of an arrangement.

Size

Use the following guidelines to select the relative size of the arrangement you want. This will help you visualize what you are giving.

Small
A small arrangement is suitable for a bedside table, bathroom, or desktop.

Medium
A medium-sized arrangement is perfect for a coffee table or side table.

Large
Request a large arrangement when size is not a limitation. It will be just right for an entryway or kitchen table.

Snapdragon

If a large arrangement is what you're after, request more foliage to add volume.

Flower Shape

There are a few basic shapes that describe flowers.

> *An assortment of different flower shapes used in an arrangement can add interest.*

Face Flower

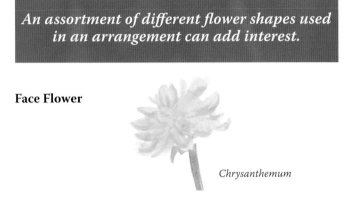

Chrysanthemum

A face flower is a large round flower on the end of a stem that adds volume or mass to an arrangement. It can be the focal point, is often the most noticeable element in the arrangement, and plays a dominant role in design. Roses, carnations, and chrysanthemums are the most common face flowers.

Filler Flower

Baby's Breath

Filler flowers are small, abundant flowers that add volume, interest, and texture to an arrangement and make it seem larger.

Form Flower

Birds of Paradise

A form flower is a unique, distinctive flower that can stand alone or act as a focal point in an arrangement so that fewer stems are needed. Examples are tropical flowers, orchids, and calla lilies.

Line Flower

Larkspur

Line flowers have long stems with flowers growing up a center stalk. They add height and are more suitable for tall arrangements. Snapdragons, delphinium, and gladiola are a few of the most popular varieties in this category.

The shape and height of the flowers will often determine the container you choose.

Finishing Touches

These elements can be used as a primary feature or as an accent in any arrangement.

Foliage
Greens play an important role in floral arrangements and can be used in abundance or not at all. There are many different choices, from light to dark, dull to shiny, and variegated to solid. Foliage is used to increase volume and stabilize the elements in an arrangement. It adds interest, texture, and color, and acts as a design accent.

For those allergic to flowers, a bouquet of mixed greens can be a perfect substitute.

Common Types of Foliage

Aspidistra
Eucalyptus
Ivy
Leather Leaf
Lemon Leaf
Myrtle
Pittosporum
Ruscus

Aspidistra

Lemon Leaf

Ivy

Berries

Many berries are available year-round, although they vary depending on the season. Berries can add color, interest, and texture and are most often used to complement an arrangement.

Hypericum

Branches

Branches, plain or flowering, can be used alone for a tall, simple appearance or to add height and interest to any arrangement.

Juniper

Flowering branches are interesting and long-lasting but often have limited availability.

Containers

Your choice of container will be influenced by the type of flowers you're using and your budget. Glass, ceramic, baskets, and novelty vessels are the most common.

Calla Lily

> *The finished height of a tall arrangement is usually one and a half to two times the height of the container.*

Tall Glass

Urn
This is the most popular vase for traditional designs. It's available in a variety of heights and sizes. Urns are suitable for many types of decor.

Cylinder or Rectangle
These containers come in a variety of heights with different size openings and are used for contemporary, high style, and simple designs. The arrangements are taller than they are wide.

> *Clear glass containers are always a good choice, but you can consider colored glass as an alternative.*

Short Glass

Short containers are quite versatile and are a perfect choice for centerpieces, side tables, or bedside tables. These arrangements are low, so they do not interfere with conversation or the line of sight at a dining table.

A low and compact arrangement may use the same number of flowers as a tall one, but will appear smaller because of the design.

Peony

Round Bowl
This simple shape comes in many different sizes. It is sometimes called an ivy bowl, rose bowl, or bubble bowl and is used for more traditional arrangements.

Cube
To create a modern, contemporary feeling, use a cube for short, low, and compact floral arrangements.

Cylinder
Similar to a cube, a cylinder is often used for shorter designs.

Ceramic

Ceramic containers are usually one of a kind. They are available in a variety of sizes, shapes, colors, and finishes: tall and short, shiny and matte, cube, cylinder, and rectangle, as well as unusual shapes.

A ceramic container hides what is inside, especially the stems and the dirty water.

Larkspur

Branches, curly willow, or foliage can add height when flowers are not tall enough.

Basket

Baskets are considered more old-fashioned and informal and are less popular than glass for floral arrangements. Floral foam is used to supply water and keep the flowers in place.

Shape
Baskets come in a variety of shapes, including oval, round, rectangle, or square, with or without a handle.

Size
Size can vary from small to large. An average basket is from six to twelve inches, regardless of shape.

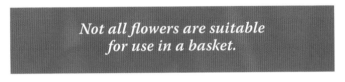

*Not all flowers are suitable
for use in a basket.*

Finishes
Baskets can be whitewashed, stained, natural, or painted a variety of colors.

Daisy

Material
Willow and vine are the most popular. Vine gives a natural, rugged appearance, and willow is smooth to the touch.

Novelty Container

Almost any container that holds water can be used for arrangements, so all you need is your imagination. Choose terra-cotta pots, metal pails, watering cans, mugs, jugs, water pitchers, bowls, or watertight boxes.

Gerbera

If cost is an important consideration, choose a smaller container. It will look better than a larger container that is not full.

Anthurium

Ceramic and novelty containers can be great keepsakes or gifts for the recipient once the flowers are gone.

VII. Basic Flower Care

These tricks of the trade will help you get more life out of your flowers. Preparation and flower care contribute to the overall health of the flowers you purchase, which makes them last longer and look better.

To maximize your budget, ask for flowers that are in season or available locally.

Lisanthus

Water is the single most important element in keeping flowers fresh. To maximize flower life, be sure your container is always filled with clean water.

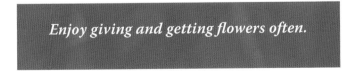

Enjoy giving and getting flowers often.

Simple Tricks of the Trade

Chrysanthemum

🎵 Make sure the container you use is clean.

🎵 Cut flower stems and change the water in the vase every two to three days and keep plenty of water in the container at all times.

🎵 Use sharp garden shears or a knife, not scissors, to cut flowers.

🎵 Cut the stems of a flower at an angle to maximize the surface area and improve water absorption.

🎵 Remove any foliage under water but leave the rest on the stem.

🎵 Use a floral preservative in the water to increase hydration.

🎵 Keep flowers as cool as possible. To lengthen their life, avoid placing them in direct sun, over air conditioning, or on a heater.

🎵 Wilted flowers can sometimes be rejuvenated with a fresh cut and submerging them in water.

VIII. The Gift of Flowers

Flowers make the perfect gift. People feel happy when they receive a gift of flowers; they also feel good about giving them.

Spider Mum

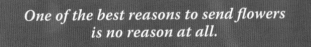

One of the best reasons to send flowers is no reason at all.

"The Home Ecology of Flowers," a study at Harvard University conducted by Nancy Etcoff, Ph.D., reveals that "people feel more compassionate towards others, have less worry and anxiety, and feel less depressed when flowers are present in the home."

An unexpected gift of flowers makes a positive impression, gives people a reason to smile, and leaves a memory that often lasts forever. You really can't go wrong when you give flowers.

Lilac

In the study "An Environmental Approach to Positive Emotion: Flowers," Dr. Jeannette Haviland-Jones, Ph.D., found that "science tells us that not only do flowers make us happier than we know but they have strong positive effects on our emotional well being."

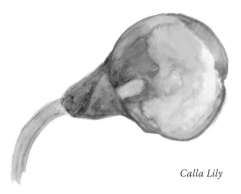

Calla Lily

Start with color. Specific colors convey different messages, and a combination of colors can create the meaning you're looking for. There are no hard and fast rules; the choices and combinations are endless. When in doubt, choose the flower colors you like best, as this will most likely please both you and the person receiving your gift.

Primary colors or informal arrangements are often more suitable for a man.

You can give flowers to celebrate any occasion (or for no reason at all) and you'll make someone feel better. Give special attention to the message you'd like to send to add impact to your gift.

> *The best way to give flowers is in a container – the flowers will most likely look better and last longer.*

Larkspur

Think about the characteristics of the person who will be receiving your gift to determine which flowers, colors, and design will be most suitable. For instance, bright, colorful flowers may be the best choice for an energetic friend, while pastels might be a better choice for someone who is more quiet or reserved. You can also match your choice of flowers and design to the decorating style of the person's home. If you know where the flowers might be placed, consider which kind of arrangement would be most appropriate for that space.

Daffodils

According to MJ Ryan, author of *Random Acts of Kindness,* "Flowers are the perfect expression of gratitude and appreciation, and they deliver a message with sincerity and care. The new research shows that these positive characteristics also are attributed to the giver. Giving flowers is an act of kindness, and the results are anything but random."

Identical arrangements will look different depending on the container you choose. Dress them up or down with vases, bowls, or baskets.

Orchid

When you give flowers, you deliver a message that your friendship or partnership is important and valued. With the simple act of giving flowers, you can leave a lasting and positive impression.

"The Power of Giving Flowers," a study at Rutgers University by Dr. Jeannette Haviland-Jones, found that "both men and women who give flowers are perceived as happy, achieving, strong, capable and courageous people."

For someone you don't know well, white flowers are a good choice. They are simple, elegant, and appropriate for any occasion or season.

I hope this guide will take some of the guesswork out of buying flowers for gift giving. With what you learn here, you can relax and feel good about the flower choices you make.

> *When you need a lift, buy flowers for yourself. You'll be surprised at how much better you'll feel.*

Snapdragon

Delphinium

Acknowledgments

Since this was my first writing endeavor, there were many people who contributed to this book. Many thanks to Nancy, who worked tirelessly to put all my ideas into a beautiful manuscript. No one could imagine the changes we made from conception to finished product. And to Claire, who kept me focused and on target with her calm and clearheaded advice.

I want to thank Steve Geruso and John Gulias, who have taught me so much about the business of flowers and design. They always encourage me but never hesitate to correct me when I make mistakes.

I am also grateful for my wonderful family, who allowed me to dwell on each and every detail of this book and believed that I could actually finish what I started. And to my mom, who always thought I could do anything if I put my mind to it.

Special thanks to my sister, Ginny, who has been my biggest fan since I started in the flower business. Without her guidance and mentoring, my life would not be the same.

Rose

References

Etcoff, Nancy. 2007. The home ecology of flowers. Boston, MA: Harvard Medical School.

Haviland-Jones, Jeannette, Terry R. McGuire, Holly Hale Rosario, and Patricia Wilson. 2005. An environmental approach to positive emotion: Flowers. *Evolutionary Psychology* 3: 104-132.

Ryan, M.J. et al. 1993. *Random Acts of Kindness*. Berkeley, CA: Conari Press.